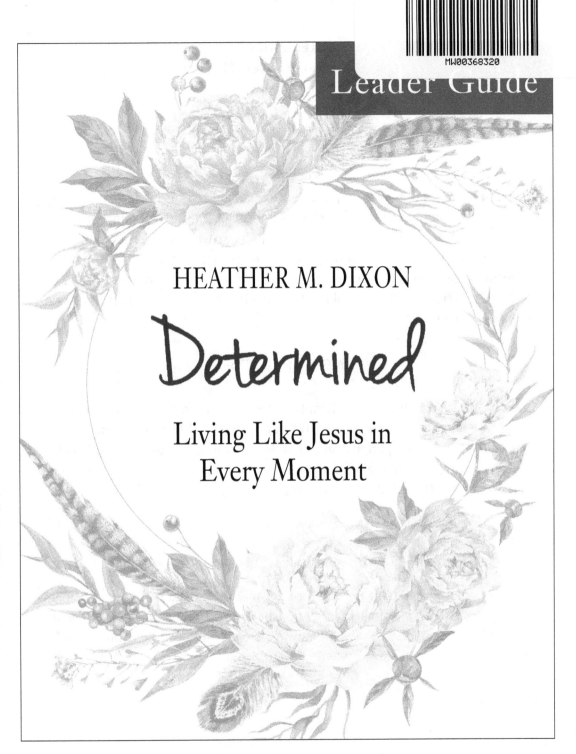

Leader Guide

HEATHER M. DIXON

Determined

Living Like Jesus in Every Moment

ABINGDON PRESS / Nashville

DETERMINED
Living Like Jesus in Every Moment
Leader Guide

Copyright © 2019 Abingdon Press
All rights reserved.

ISBN 978-1-5018-7888-6

19 20 21 22 23 24 25 26 27 28—10 9 8 7 6 5 4 3 2 1
MANUFACTURED IN THE UNITED STATES OF AMERICA

Contents

About the Author

Heather M. Dixon is an author, speaker, and Bible teacher who understands living with a story that is not easy. Diagnosed with an incurable and terminal genetic disorder that she inherited from her mother, she is passionate about encouraging and equipping women to trust in God, face their greatest fears, and live with hope, especially in the midst of difficult circumstances. When she is not blogging at The Rescued Letters or speaking at women's conferences and events, Heather loves to make the most of everyday moments such as cooking for her husband and son, brainstorming all the possible ways to organize Legos and superheroes, checking out way too many library books, or unashamedly indulging in her love for all things Disney. Heather is the author of *Determined: Living Like Jesus in Every Moment*, *Ready: Finding the Courage to Face the Unknown* and a regular contributor to *Journey* magazine.

Follow Heather:

🐦 @rescuedletters

📷 @rescuedletters

📘 @rescuedletters

📌 @rescuedletters

Her blog: therescuedletters.com
        (check here also for event dates and booking information)

Introduction

For most of us, life is busy and filled with distractions, pulling us in every way but God's way. Sometimes the most challenging thing we have to do is simply stay the course.

When we're driven by distraction, it's easy to wander through life without appreciating the gift of every moment we've been given. And when we overlook the rich rewards of walking hand in hand with Jesus, the result is an unsatisfying life, missed opportunities to experience the joy of being in sync with God, and days marked with apathy and anxiety instead of passion and peace. Our time on earth is measured. We should want to make every moment count—not only because we aren't guaranteed the next one but also because this is exactly how our Savior spent His time here.

How, then, do we walk out unwavering joy-filled faith every day, determined to let go of the things that keep us from experiencing abundant life and fulfilling the plans God has for us? The answers are found in following the footsteps of the One who lived fully, because He was determined that we might do the same.

In this six-week study of Luke, we will follow the life and ministry of Jesus as we consider the choices He made on His way to the cross. We'll intimately connect with a Savior who remained laser-focused on His mission to love the world. In return, we'll receive a model for intentional living that we can replicate to ensure we are living each day to the fullest and making a difference for God's kingdom. And together we'll determine to embrace the abundant life we are promised in Jesus.

About the Participant Book

Before the first session, you will want to distribute copies of the participant book to the members of your group. Be sure to communicate that they are to complete the first week of readings before your first group session. For each week there are five readings or lessons that combine study of Scripture with personal reflection and application (boldface type indicates write-in-the-book questions and activities).

On average you will need about twenty to thirty minutes to complete each lesson. Completing these readings each week will prepare the women for the discussion and activities of the group session.

About This Leader Guide

As you gather each week with the members of your group, you will have the opportunity to watch the video, discuss and respond to what you're learning, and pray together. You will need access to a television and DVD player with working remotes.

Creating a warm and inviting atmosphere will help to make the women feel welcome. Although optional, you might consider providing snacks for your first meeting and inviting group members to rotate in bringing refreshments each week.

This leader guide and the DVD will be your primary tools for leading your group on this journey to learn intentional, determined living after the example of Jesus. In this book you will find outlines for six group sessions, each formatted for either a 60-minute or 90-minute group session:

60-Minute Format
Welcome/Opening Prayer (3 minutes)
Icebreaker (5 minutes)
Group-Centering Video (1–2 minutes, optional)
Content Video (7–10 minutes)
Group Discussion (30 minutes)
Prayer Requests (5–10 minutes)

90-Minute Format
Welcome/Opening Prayer (5–8 minutes)
Icebreaker (5 minutes)
Group-Centering Video (1–2 minutes, optional)
Content Video (7–10 minutes)
Group Discussion (40 minutes)
Determined Conversation (10–15 minutes)
Prayer Requests (5–1o minutes)

As you can see, the basic elements remain the same in each format: a welcome time and opening prayer, an "icebreaker" question that everyone can answer, a group-centering video to help participants focus their hearts and minds on God and God's Word (optional—see page 9 for more information), a content video segment, group discussion, and prayer time. The 90-minute option offers longer times for fellowship, discussion, and prayer plus Determined Conversation time for smaller groups of two to three people. If you choose not to do the Determined Conversation, you may add that time to another element of the session, such as group discussion or prayer. Feel free to adapt or modify either of these formats, as well as the individual segments and activities, in any way to meet the specific needs and preferences of your group.

Before You Begin

If the burdens you carry ever pose a threat to your peace, you're in the right place. My prayer is that through our time together Jesus will reveal to you that the burdens you carry do not determine your capacity for contentment or your ability to make a kingdom impact for Christ. Rather, in spite of whatever life throws your way, you can determine to live like Jesus—living abundantly in every moment!

Heather

About Group Centering

Our lives are often busy and hectic as we rush from one activity or event to another, juggling more balls than we can keep in the air. You may find that participants are rushed and distracted as they arrive at Bible study—yourself included. You've had to pull away from your busy schedules to get there. Playing the Group Centering video after the icebreaker and before the Group Teaching video will allow you to disconnect from the outside world and center your minds and hearts on God and God's Word.

Each video is approximately two minutes long and leads the group through the following exercise:

1. First, you are instructed to take a moment to let go of the cares of your day by taking several slow, deep breaths and relaxing your body.
2. Next you are guided to say a prayer, thanking God for His presence and love and inviting Him to prepare your heart and mind to receive God's Word.
3. After this you are invited to read a Scripture verse slowly, reflecting upon it. (The verse used is the Focus Verse for the week.)
4. Following the Scripture, there are several brief summary statements to conclude this reflective time.

Encourage group members to sit quietly through the duration of the video, focusing their minds and hearts on God and God's Word. After the Group Centering time, there is no need for discussion. You may proceed immediately to the Group Teaching video.

If this exercise is not a fit for your group or you do not have time to include it, simply begin with the Group Teaching video. You know your group better than anyone and are encouraged to customize your group session to meet their needs and interests.

Leader Helps

Preparing for the Sessions

- Check out your meeting space before each group session. Make sure the room is ready. Do you have enough chairs? Do you have the equipment and supplies you need? (See the list of materials needed in each session outline.)
- Pray for your group and each group member by name. Ask God to work in the life of every woman in your group.
- Read and complete the week's readings in the participant book and review the session outline in the leader guide. Put a check mark beside the discussion questions you want to cover and make any notes in the margins that you want to share in your discussion time.

Leading the Sessions

- Personally greet each woman as she arrives. If desired, take attendance. (This will assist you in identifying members who have missed several sessions so that you may contact them and let them know they were missed.)
- At the start of each session, ask the women to turn off or silence their cell phones.
- Always start on time. Honor the efforts of those who are on time.
- Encourage everyone to participate fully, but don't put anyone on the spot. Invite the women to share as they are comfortable. Be prepared to offer a personal example or answer if no one else responds at first.

- Facilitate but don't dominate. Remember that if you talk most of the time, group members may tend to listen passively rather than to engage personally.
- Try not to interrupt, judge, or minimize anyone's comments or input.
- Remember that you are not expected to be the expert or have all the answers. Acknowledge that all of you are on this journey together, with the Holy Spirit as your leader and guide. If issues or questions arise that you don't feel equipped to answer or handle, talk with the pastor or a staff member at your church.
- Encourage good discussion, but don't be timid about calling time on a particular question and moving ahead. Part of your responsibility is to keep the group on track. If you decide to spend extra time on a given question or activity, consider skipping or spending less time on another question or activity in order to stay on schedule.
- Try to end on time. If you are running over, give members the opportunity to leave if they need to. Then wrap up as quickly as you can.
- Be prepared for some women to want to hang out and talk at the end. If you need everyone to leave by a certain time, communicate this at the beginning of the session. If you are meeting in a church during regularly scheduled activities or have arranged for childcare, be sensitive to the agreed upon ending time.
- Thank the women for coming, and let them know you're looking forward to seeing them next time.

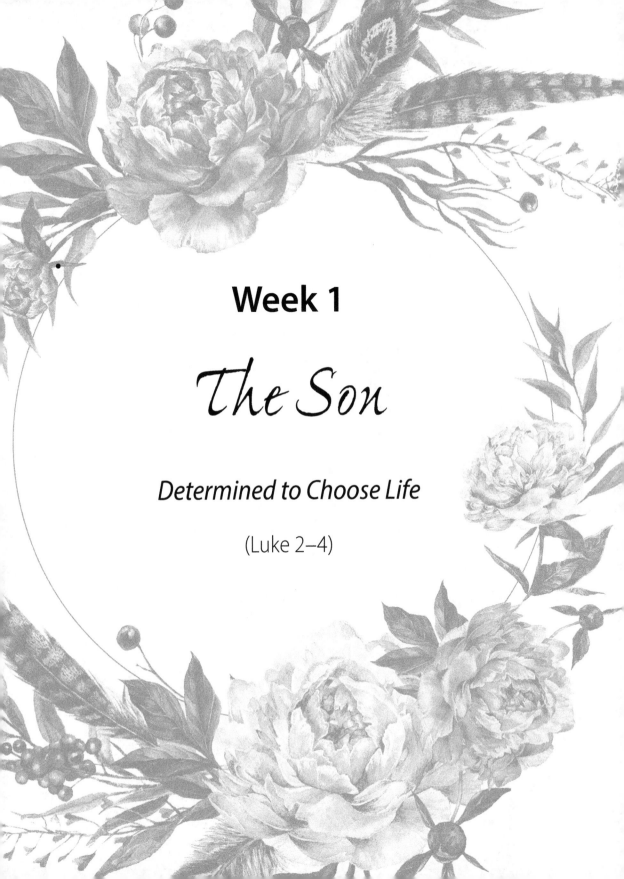

Week 1

The Son

Determined to Choose Life

(Luke 2–4)

Leader Prep

Focus Verse

Therefore be imitators of God, as beloved children.

(*Ephesians* 5:1 ESV)

Scripture Highlights

Day 1

[36]*There was also a prophet, Anna, the daughter of Penuel, of the tribe of Asher. She was very old; she had lived with her husband seven years after her marriage,* [37]*and then was a widow until she was eighty-four. She never left the temple but worshiped night and day, fasting and praying.* [38]*Coming up to them at that very moment, she gave thanks to God and spoke about the child to all who were looking forward to the redemption of Jerusalem.*

(Luke 2:36-38)

Day 2

[49]*"Why were you searching for me?" he asked. "Didn't you know I had to be in my Father's house?"* [52] *. . . And Jesus grew in wisdom and stature, and in favor with God and man.*

(Luke 2:49-52)

Day 3

[21]*When all the people were being baptized, Jesus was baptized too. And as he was praying, heaven was opened* [22]*and the Holy Spirit descended on him in bodily form like a dove. And a voice came from heaven: "You are my Son, whom I love; with you I am well pleased."*

(Luke 3:21-22)

Day 4

[1]*Jesus, full of the Holy Spirit, left the Jordan and was led by the Spirit into the wilderness,* [2]*where for forty days he was tempted by the devil.*

(Luke 4:1-2)

<u>Day 5</u>

[18]*"The Spirit of the Lord is on me,*
  because he has anointed me
  to proclaim good news to the poor.
He has sent me to proclaim freedom for the prisoners
  and recovery of sight for the blind,
to set the oppressed free,
  [19]*to proclaim the year of the Lord's favor."*

(Luke 4:18-19)

Materials Needed

- Determined DVD and DVD player
- Stick-on name tags and markers (optional)

Session Outline

Note: Refer to the format templates on page 6 for suggested time allotments.

Welcome and Opening Prayer

Offer a word of welcome to the group and a brief opening prayer, asking God to prepare the group to receive His Word and hear His voice.

Icebreaker

Invite the women to respond briefly to the following prompt:

- Share a time when you were especially determined.

Video

Two short video segments are provided for Week 1. You are encouraged to begin with the group centering video to help participants slow down internally, disconnect from the distractions of their busy lives, and center their hearts on God and God's Word. Then play the content video segment, which distills and recaps the main takeaways of the week's lessons. Invite participants to complete the Video Viewer Guide for Week 1 in the participant book as they watch (page 41). (Answers are provided on page 200 of the participant workbook and 63 of this leader guide.)

Group Discussion

Video Discussion Questions

- Are you living with something that feels impossible?
- If so, what would it mean for you to choose life with Jesus in the midst of it?

Participant Book Discussion Questions

Note: More questions are provided than you will have time to cover. Put a check mark beside those you would like your group to discuss. Page references are provided for those questions that relate to questions or activities in the participant book.

Day 1: Witness to Worship

- We are our most beautiful when our faces are turned toward the heavens in praise of who God is and all that He has done for us. Do you have a habit of worship? If so, describe it. If not, consider and discuss what a habit of worship might look like based on the verses listed on page 15 of the participant workbook.

- How have you seen the act of worship positively change your life? If you can't think of any examples, how might a consistent habit of worship impact your day-to-day attitude? (page 16)
- Read Luke 2:36-38 aloud. How do we know from what we've read and studied about Anna that she was determined to worship her King against all odds? Can you recall a time when the choice to worship God conflicted with what was expected of you? If so, how did you respond? (page 17)
- How might you embrace a worshipful heart? (page 18)

Notes:

Day 2: Finding Wisdom in the Word

- Read aloud Luke 2:41-52. How do you imagine Mary and Joseph felt when they found Jesus in the Temple? How does Jesus' reply to his parents in verse 49 echo the divine truth shared by Simeon and Anna (page 21)?
- Can you remember a time when God spoke something so clearly that it was impossible to doubt His voice? Perhaps it was a verse that leaped off the pages of the Bible, an answer to a heartfelt prayer, or a gut-conviction that you needed to do something specific in order to obey God. (page 21)
- If we want to retain what God speaks, we'll have to determine to keep returning to Him. What are some ways that we return to God over and over again?
- Read Proverbs 4:1-13 aloud. What sticks out to you in these verses about gleaning wisdom? (page 23)

Notes:

Day 3: A Promise to Pray

- Think back to a moment in your life when everything changed. What ended? Did something begin in its place? What were the new rules? How did you respond to the change? Was God a part of your response? Was prayer? (pages 24–25)
- Read Luke 3:21-22 aloud. What happened when Jesus prayed? Do you think it was a coincidence that these things happened as Jesus was praying? Why or why not? (page 27)
- The Savior of the world was on His knees before the start of something that changed everything. As we think about His example, let's consider our own prayer lives. Do you have a habit of prayer? Is it consistent? Sporadic? Heartfelt? Need-based? How would you describe your current prayer life? (page 28)
- If what you just described didn't include words such as *consistent*, *rewarding*, or *regular*, what would it take for you to start defining prayer as *required*—not in the sense of an expectation or obligation but in the sense of a necessity for daily life? What perspective shift do you need in order to move the habit of prayer from a rote behavior you are simply checking off the list to an absolute necessity for your potential to thrive as a follower of Jesus?

Notes:

Day 4: An Obligation to Obey

- Again and again, God's Word reminds us that the pain we experience today can be used to prepare us for our god-designed purpose. So, how do we bridge the gap between what we see and what lies ahead? How have you experienced the tension between the pain of today and the hope found in tomorrow? What sustains you?
- Read Hebrews 4:15 aloud. Not unlike those who undergo first aid training to assist someone in a medical crisis, Jesus undergoes humanity training in the wilderness to assist us in a spiritual crisis. What does it mean to you personally that Jesus has experience with our humanity?

- What are the three Ps of the wilderness—the three temptations Jesus faced? (pages 31–32)
- Consider for a moment the thought patterns running through your head during seasons of hardship. Do you ever find yourself struggling with questions or doubts related to God's provision or power or wanting to handle things yourself without God? If so, share briefly.

Notes:

Day 5: Determined Patterns of Faith

- Jesus was determined to fulfill His purpose from the start. Read Luke 4:18-19 aloud. What are the five intentions of Jesus' earthly ministry named in these verses? (page 36)
- Of the five intentions Jesus mentioned, which one resonates most with you today? Why? (page 37)
- Read Proverbs 16:9; Isaiah 43:7; and Ephesians 2:10 aloud. What do these verses say about our God-given purpose? (page 39)
- How does it feel to know that God isn't looking for perfect people who know how to do everything right but for people who are willing to choose habits of faithfulness? What does this mean to you?

Notes:

Determined Conversation

Divide into groups of 2-3 for the following:

- Take turns sharing the God-given purpose you wrote on page 39, and the ways you can deepen your determination to practice the daily habits of Worship, Word, Pray, and Obey. (page 40)

Prayer Requests

Close the session by taking personal prayer requests from group members and leading the group in prayer. As you progress to later weeks in the study, you might encourage members to participate in the Closing Prayer by praying out loud for one another and the requests given.

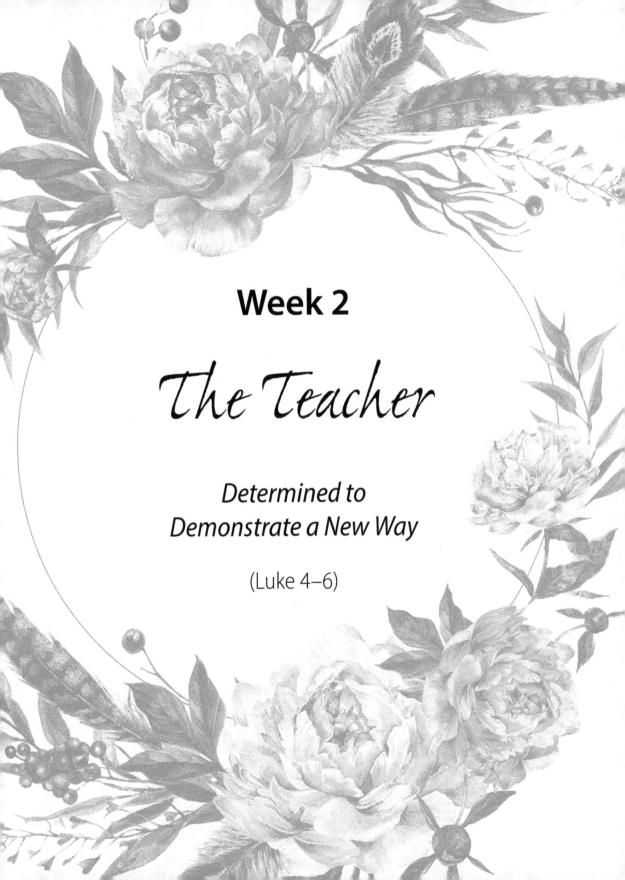

Week 2

The Teacher

Determined to Demonstrate a New Way

(Luke 4–6)

Leader Prep

Focus Verse

¹In the beginning was the Word, and the Word was with God, and the Word was God. ²He was with God in the beginning. ³Through him all things were made; without him nothing was made that has been made. ⁴In him was life, and that life was the light of all mankind.

(John 1:1-4)

Scripture Highlights

Day 1

⁴²At daybreak, Jesus went out to a solitary place.

(Luke 4:42)

Day 2

⁴When he had finished speaking, he said to Simon, "Put out into deep water, and let down the nets for a catch."

⁵Simon answered, "Master, we've worked hard all night and haven't caught anything. But because you say so, I will let down the nets."

⁶When they had done so, they caught such a large number of fish that their nets began to break."

(Luke 5:4-6)

Day 3

²⁹Then Levi held a great banquet for Jesus at his house, and a large crowd of tax collectors and others were eating with them. ³⁰But the Pharisees and the teachers of the law who belonged to their sect complained to his disciples, "Why do you eat and drink with tax collectors and sinners?"

³¹Jesus answered them, "It is not the healthy who need a doctor, but the sick.

(Luke 5:29-31)

Day 4

²⁰Looking at his disciples, he said:

*"Blessed are you who are poor,
    for yours is the kingdom of God.*

^{21}Blessed are you who hunger now,
     for you will be satisfied.
Blessed are you who weep now,
     for you will laugh.
^{22}Blessed are you when people hate you . . .
     because of the Son of Man.

               (Luke 6:20-22)

<u>Day 5</u>

^{27}"But to you who are listening I say: Love your enemies, do good to those who hate you, ^{28}bless those who curse you, pray for those who mistreat you."

               (Luke 6:27-28)

Materials Needed

- *Determined* DVD and DVD player
- Stick-on name tags and markers (optional)

Session Outline

Note: Refer to the format templates on page 6 for suggested time allotments.

Welcome and Opening Prayer

Offer a word of welcome to the group and a brief opening prayer, asking God to prepare the group to receive His Word and hear His voice.

Icebreaker

Invite the women to share short responses to the following question:

- When was the last time you learned something new? What was it?

Video

Two short video segments are provided for Week 2. You are encouraged to begin with the group-centering video to help participants slow down internally, disconnect from the distractions of their busy lives, and center their hearts on God and God's Word. Then play the content video segment, which distills and recaps the main takeaways of the week's lessons. Invite participants to complete the Video Viewer Guide for Week 2 in the participant book as they watch (page 73). (Answers are provided on page 200 of the participant workbook and 63 of this leader guide.)

Group Discussion

Video Discussion Questions

- How can we store up God's good in our hearts?
- What would it look like for you to be an overflowing pitcher of God's truth and love in your everyday world?

Participant Book Discussion Questions

Note: More questions are provided than you will have time to cover. Put a check mark beside those you would like your group to discuss. Page references are provided for those questions that relate to questions or activities in the participant book.

Day 1: A Solitary Place

- Read aloud Luke 4:31-44. According to this passage, what was a typical day like for Jesus? (Refer to the sequence of events on pages 45-46.)
- Consider your daily obligations for this week. Would you define your schedule as busy, relaxed, or somewhere in between? (page 45)

- Although He was completely divine, Jesus knew what it felt like to be fully human. When we are tempted to think that no one could possibly understand how stressed out, exhausted, or weary we are, we can follow Jesus' footsteps to solitude. When was the last time you deliberately stopped what you were doing to rest? Describe what that looked like for you and how you felt afterward.
- Why do you think silence and solitude are essential to living out our mission? What are some ways you are planning to incorporate more time for silence and solitude?

Notes:

Day 2: Strength in Numbers

- Read aloud Luke 5:5. How does this verse imply that Simon is familiar with Jesus' authority? (page 50)
- The word *disciple* is used fifty times in the Book of Luke, although he does not introduce the word formally until Luke 5:30. How would you define *disciple* in your own words? (page 51)
- Where does Jesus direct Simon Peter to go in Luke 5:4? (page 52) Like Peter, Jesus allows ordinary men and women like us to do extraordinary things when we trust in His authority over our lives. Can you recall a time when Jesus led you into a situation that felt like it was over your head or out of your comfort zone? (page 52)
- Read aloud Luke 5:9-11. Who else is called to be a disciple on this occasion? Do you find it easier to obey God alone or in the community of others? Why? (page 53)
- God intends for the real work of His kingdom to be done in the collective. In what ways are you already collaborating with others to serve Jesus in your church, community, or world? (page 55)

Notes:

Day 3: A Friend of Sinners

- Read Luke 5:30 aloud. What was the implication? Can you recall a time when you have been asked a similar question? Refer to your answer on page 58.
- Does it surprise you that Jesus often chose to eat with sinners and outcasts? Why or why not?
- What would you say your comfort level is with dining with those who would be considered outcasts today?
- Jesus is a party-thrower and a party-goer. He celebrates everyone who comes to repentance, including us. What's more, He intentionally seeks out those who need Him. What are some ways that you could become a party-thrower and party-goer, one who seeks out people who need Jesus?

Notes:

Day 4: The Upside-Down Kingdom

- Read Luke 6:20-22 aloud. What would you say it means to be blessed? In what ways is the word *blessed* sometimes misunderstood?
- How did Jesus define what it means to be blessed? Review your answers in the chart on page 64.
- Read John 10:10 aloud. Does Jesus' teaching on the blessed life [in Luke 6] align with your definition of abundant life? Why or why not? (page 65)
- The presence of blessing is defined by our faith in God's reality, not our own. How could the way Jesus defines blessing give us a new perspective when we face challenges and difficulties?

Notes:

Day 5: Reflective Love

- Read Luke 6:27-31 aloud. According to Jesus' explanation of loving your enemies, what might it look like for us to love our enemies today? Share some practical examples. (pages 70–71)
- How can loving our enemies benefit both others and ourselves? (page 72)
- What did you learn about the difference between self-care and soul-care? Would you say you are better at one than the other? What are some ways that you practice Sabbath rest?
- Though there certainly is a time for self-care or soul-care, followers of Jesus are called to a higher standard of putting others' needs before our own as He did. How do you balance your own needs and the call to put others first as Jesus did?
- If we want to truly live like Jesus, we'll have to pursue our enemies with agape love—selfless, unconditional, forgiving, and relentless love. What does it mean to pursue your enemies? Do you find this easy or difficult? Why?

Notes:

Determined Conversation

Divide into groups of 2-3 for the following:

- Share your responses in the chart on page 64 regarding times when you were blessed to be poor, hungry, sorrowful, and persecuted. How did Jesus respond to you in those times?

Prayer Requests

Close the session by taking personal prayer requests from group members and leading the group in prayer. As you progress to later weeks in the study, you might encourage members to participate in the Closing Prayer by praying out loud for one another and the requests given.

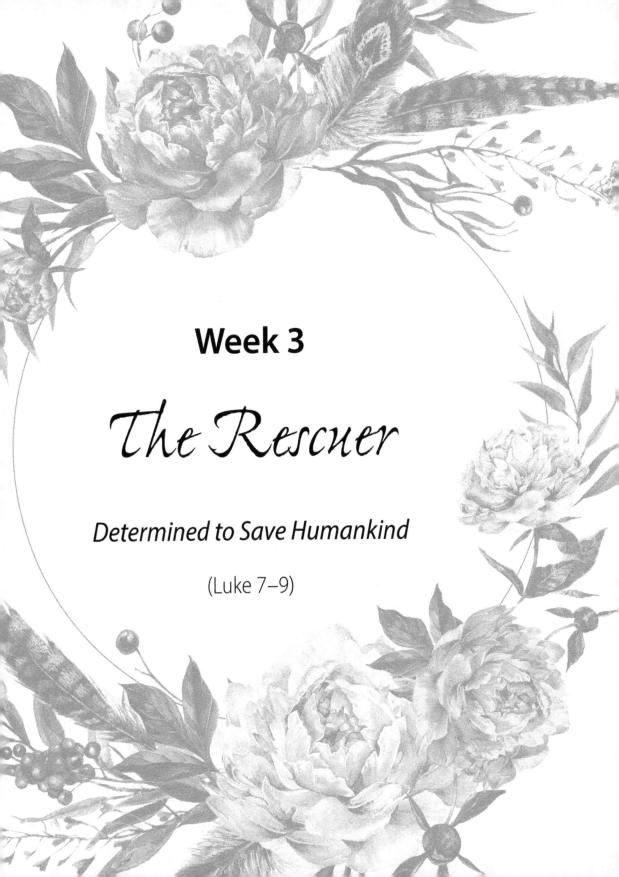

Week 3

The Rescuer

Determined to Save Humankind

(Luke 7–9)

Leader Prep

Focus Verse

4What is man that you are mindful of him,
   and the son of man that you care for him?
5Yet you have made him a little lower than the heavenly beings
   and crowned him with glory and honor.

(Psalm 8:4-5 ESV)

Scripture Highlights

Day 1

12As he approached the town gate, a dead person was being carried out—the only son of his mother, and she was a widow. And a large crowd from the town was with her. 13When the Lord saw her, his heart went out to her and he said, "Don't cry."

(Luke 7:12-13)

Day 2

37A woman in that town who lived a sinful life learned that Jesus was eating at the Pharisee's house, so she came there with an alabaster jar of perfume. 38As she stood behind him at his feet weeping, she began to wet his feet with her tears. Then she wiped them with her hair, kissed them and poured perfume on them.

(Luke 7:37-38)

Day 3

27When Jesus stepped ashore, he was met by a demon-possessed man from the town.... 28When he saw Jesus, he cried out and fell at his feet, shouting at the top of his voice, "What do you want with me, Jesus, Son of the Most High God? I beg you, don't torture me!"

30. . . Jesus asked him, "What is your name?"

"Legion," he replied, because many demons had gone into him. 31And they begged Jesus repeatedly not to order them to go into the Abyss.

32A large herd of pigs was feeding there on the hillside. The demons begged Jesus to let them go into the pigs, and he gave them permission. 33When the demons came out of the man, they went into the pigs, and the herd rushed down the steep bank into the lake and was drowned.

(Luke 8:27-28, 30-33)

<u>Day 4</u>

[41]*Then a man named Jairus, a synagogue leader, came and fell at Jesus' feet, pleading with him to come to his house* [42]*because his only daughter, a girl of about twelve, was dying.*

As Jesus was on his way, the crowds almost crushed him. [43]*And a woman was there who had been subject to bleeding for twelve years, but no one could heal her.* [44]*She came up behind him and touched the edge of his cloak, and immediately her bleeding stopped.*

(Luke 8:41-44)

<u>Day 5</u>

[16]*Taking the five loaves and the two fish and looking up to heaven, he gave thanks and broke them. Then he gave them to the disciples to distribute to the people.* [17]*They all ate and were satisfied, and the disciples picked up twelve basketfuls of broken pieces that were left over.*

(Luke 9:16-17)

Materials Needed

- *Determined* DVD and DVD player
- Stick-on name tags and markers (optional)

Session Outline

Note: Refer to the format templates on page 6 for suggested time allotments.

Welcome and Opening Prayer

Offer a word of welcome to the group and a brief opening prayer, asking God to prepare the group to receive His Word and hear His voice.

Icebreaker

Invite the women to share short responses to the following question:

- When have you needed to be rescued?

Video

Two short video segments are provided for Week 3. You are encouraged to begin with the group-centering video to help participants slow down internally, disconnect from the distractions of their busy lives, and center their hearts on God and God's Word. Then play the content video segment, which distills and recaps the main takeaways of the week's lessons. Invite participants to complete the Video Viewer Guide for Week 3 in the participant book as they watch (page 106). (Answers are provided on page 200 of the participant workbook and 63 of this leader guide.)

Group Discussion

Video Discussion Questions

- What is keeping you from abundant living?
- If you were to tell God about your faith, rather than your fears, what would you say?

Participant Book Discussion Questions

Note: More questions are provided than you will have time to cover. Put a check mark beside those you would like your group to discuss. Page references are provided for those questions that relate to questions or activities in the participant book.

Day 1: Rescue from Grief (Determined to Be Compassionate)

- Would you describe yourself as a compassionate person? Why or why not? (page 78)
- Read Luke 7:13. What actions does Jesus take in response to seeing the mother with compassion? Why do you think Jesus was compassionate toward this mother? (pages 78–79)

- If you are comfortable sharing, what is your greatest source of grief today? (page 80) How have friends lifted you up in this struggle? In what ways have you experienced compassion?

Notes:

Day 2: Rescue from Sin (Determined to Be Devoted)

- How would you explain what "soul rest" is? Can you recall a time when you craved rest for your soul? (page 83)
- Read Galatians 5:22-23 aloud. What are the benefits or fruit of communion with God? Is there a particular area you struggle with? (pages 83–84)
- When you have sinned, do you find it easy or difficult to respond to Jesus with the same attitude of humility as the woman who anointed him? (page 85)
- Read Luke 7:50. What does Jesus say to the woman? What does it feel like to "go in peace" after you've been forgiven from a sin struggle?

Notes:

Day 3: Rescue from Chains (Determined to Leave a Legacy)

- When you think of the term *abundant life*, what comes to mind? (page 89)
- Besides anxiety, what else might get in the way of Jesus' promise of living fully? Would you define your way of life today as abundant? Why or why not? (page 90)
- According to the Scriptures on page 90, what is abundant living in Jesus? (page 91)

- Jesus makes you worthy of influence. So, what kind of legacy are you leaving? What legacy do you hope to leave behind?

Notes:

Day 4: Rescue from Unbelief (Determined to Possess Unwavering Faith)
- What is your story of coming to know Jesus?
- Read Luke 8:47-48 aloud. What is Jesus' response to the woman? (page 96)
- When and how has Jesus healed you of something, whether physical or emotional? How does it feel knowing that you cannot go unnoticed by Jesus? (page 96)
- Do you think there is a difference between *believing in God* and *believing God*? Why or why not? (page 97)
- Have you experienced a time of waiting for God to answer a prayer and wondering if you'd ever get an answer? Or maybe you even wanted to give up talking to Jesus about it anymore. If so, tell about that time.

Notes:

Day 5: Rescue from Apathy (Determined to Solve Problems)
- Would you say you operate mostly out of your own strength or Jesus' strength? How could you lean into Jesus' strength more and more?
- Read Luke 9:12 aloud. How do the disciples respond to the influx of crowds? What factors do you think are at play with their request to send the crowd away? (page 102)
- When you are tired and weary, how concerned do you tend to be for the needs of others? Have you ever been so depleted that you had nothing left to give? If so, give a brief example.

- Jesus always works from a place of abundance. He will always have more than enough of what you need. Tell about a time when Jesus was more than enough of what you needed at a particular moment.

Notes:

Determined Conversation

Divide into groups of 2-3 for the following:

- Share the specific needs that you identified and how you will fill them (page 105). Then pray for one another related to these areas.

Prayer Requests

Close the session by taking personal prayer requests from group members and leading the group in prayer. As you progress to later weeks in the study, you might encourage members to participate in the Closing Prayer by praying out loud for one another and the requests given.

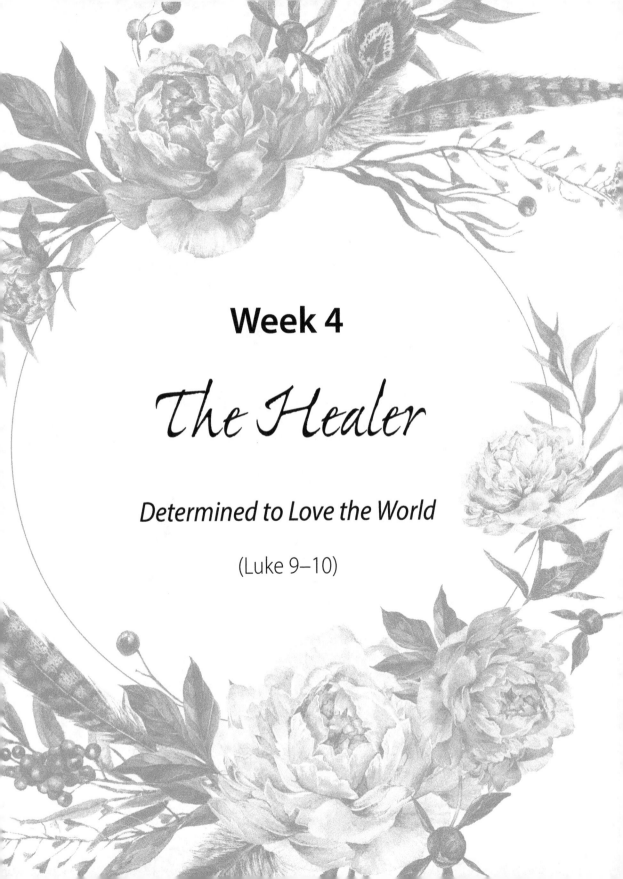

Week 4

The Healer

Determined to Love the World

(Luke 9–10)

Leader Prep

Focus Verse

¹Since we are surrounded by such a great cloud of witnesses, let us throw off everything that hinders and the sin that so easily entangles. And let us run with perseverance the race marked out for us, ²fixing our eyes on Jesus, the pioneer and perfecter of faith. For the joy set before him he endured the cross, scorning its shame, and sat down at the right hand of the throne of God.

(Hebrews 12:1-2)

Scripture Highlights

Day 1

¹⁸Once when Jesus was praying in private and his disciples were with him, he asked them, "Who do the crowds say I am?"

²⁰ . . . Peter answered, "God's Messiah."

(Luke 9:18, 20b)

Day 2

²³"Whoever wants to be my disciple must deny themselves and take up their cross daily and follow me. ²⁴For whoever wants to save their life will lose it, but whoever loses their life for me will save it."

(Luke 9:23-24)

Day 3

⁵¹As the time approached for him to be taken up to heaven, Jesus resolutely set out for Jerusalem.

(Luke 9:51)

Day 4

³⁰ . . . "A man was going down from Jerusalem to Jericho, when he was attacked by robbers. . . . ³³But a Samaritan, as he traveled, came where the man was; and when he saw him, he took pity on him. ³⁴He went to him and bandaged his wounds, pouring on oil and wine. Then he put the man on his own donkey, brought him to an inn and took care of him."

(Luke 10:30-34)

<u>Day 5</u>

[41]"Martha, Martha," the Lord answered, "you are worried and upset about many things, [42]but few things are needed—or indeed only one. Mary has chosen what is better, and it will not be taken away from her."

(Luke 10:41-42)

Materials Needed

- Determined DVD and DVD player
- Stick-on name tags and markers (optional)

Session Outline

Note: Refer to the format templates on page 6 for suggested time allotments.

Welcome and Opening Prayer

Offer a word of welcome to the group and a brief opening prayer, asking God to prepare the group to receive His Word and hear His voice.

Icebreaker

Invite the women to share short responses to the following prompt:

- Tell of a time when your expectations were turned upside down— when things didn't go as you planned or hoped.

Video

Two short video segments are provided for Week 4. You are encouraged to begin with the group-centering video to help participants slow down internally, disconnect from the distractions of their busy lives, and center their hearts on God and God's Word. Then play the content video segment, which distills and recaps the main takeaways of the week's lessons. Invite participants to complete the Video Viewer Guide for Week 4 in the participant book as they watch (page 137). (Answers are provided on page 200 of the participant workbook and 63 of this leader guide.)

Group Discussion

Video Discussion Questions

- Is there something about your story that you don't like? How do you need Jesus' rescue?

Participant Book Discussion Questions

Note: More questions are provided than you will have time to cover. Put a check mark beside those you would like your group to discuss. Page references are provided for those questions that relate to questions or activities in the participant book.

Day 1: Healing Our Past

- Read Luke 9:18-20 aloud. What were three identities for Jesus that people in his day talked about? Who does Peter say Jesus is in verse 20? (pages 111–112)

- What does our world say about Jesus? How does our society view Jesus today? (page 111)
- To embrace abundant life and our future with Christ, we must be willing to let Him heal our past. What has Jesus healed you from so that you might walk into abundant life? Is there something from your past that still needs healing from Jesus today? (page 114)
- Jesus is in the business of daily do-overs, and He's rather fond of second chances that are rooted in His grace. When have you experienced a do-over or a second chance lately? How did God work in your life to bring about this do-over or second chance?

Notes:

Day 2: Embracing Our Present

- Read Luke 9:22-23 aloud. What four things did Jesus say would happen to Him? What are three requirements of a disciple? (pages 116–117)
- When we choose to follow Jesus like the disciples, we trade the known of the world for the unknown of life with Christ. And letting go of our expectations isn't easy. When have your expectations been turned upside down? (page 116)
- Read Acts 20:24 and Galatians 2:20. What expectations do you have about your own life? What are your dreams, goals, and aspirations, and how do they align with these verses? (page 119)
- While we're waiting on the coming Kingdom, how can we live with joy now when life before us fails to meet our expectations?

Notes:

Day 3: Transforming Our Future

- Read Luke 9:51 aloud from several different translations. Why is this a key verse for our study?
- Determined living is about setting our face like flint, stiffening ourselves toward the challenges that lie ahead while softening our hearts toward the hope that is found in Jesus. What lies ahead for you that will need an extra dose of determination to see it through? (page 124)
- How might what you are facing serve a greater purpose for God's kingdom? (page 125)
- Determining to live like Jesus will transform us into messengers of hope in a dark and broken world. What are some ways to be messengers of hope in a dark and broken world that you are excited about?

Notes:

Day 4: Refining Our Comfort Zones

- How would you define a good Samaritan? (refer to page 127)
- It is possible that in the parable of the good Samaritan, both the priest and the Levite were concerned with the risk of ritual impurity by touching a seemingly dead body. But Jesus implies that they were simply looking for loopholes in the command to love their neighbor as themselves. Do you ever find yourself looking for loopholes in what God has commanded you? If so, what is an example? (Don't worry, this is a no-judgment zone!) (page 129)
- Can you think of a specific situation where this lesson from the Samaritan could be applied in your neighborhood, city, or state? (page 130)

Notes:

Day 5: Aligning Our Hearts

- Read aloud the story of Mary and Martha found in Luke 10:38-42. How does Jesus respond to Martha's outcry, and how does His response to her affect your sense of fairness? (page 133)
- Why is Mary's choice the better one? (page 133)
- Why do works performed without devotion only lead to resentment, and when have you experienced this?
- How can we be sure that we are working out of the overflow of sitting at Jesus' feet and not just out of duty or a need to perform?

Notes:

Determined Conversation

Divide into groups of 2-3 for the following:

- Review the "7 Practical Ways to Choose Life Every Day" on pages 135–136. Which of these choices do you need to work on most, and how might you do that?

Prayer Requests

Close the session by taking personal prayer requests from group members and leading the group in prayer. Encourage members to participate in the Closing Prayer by praying out loud for one another and the requests given.

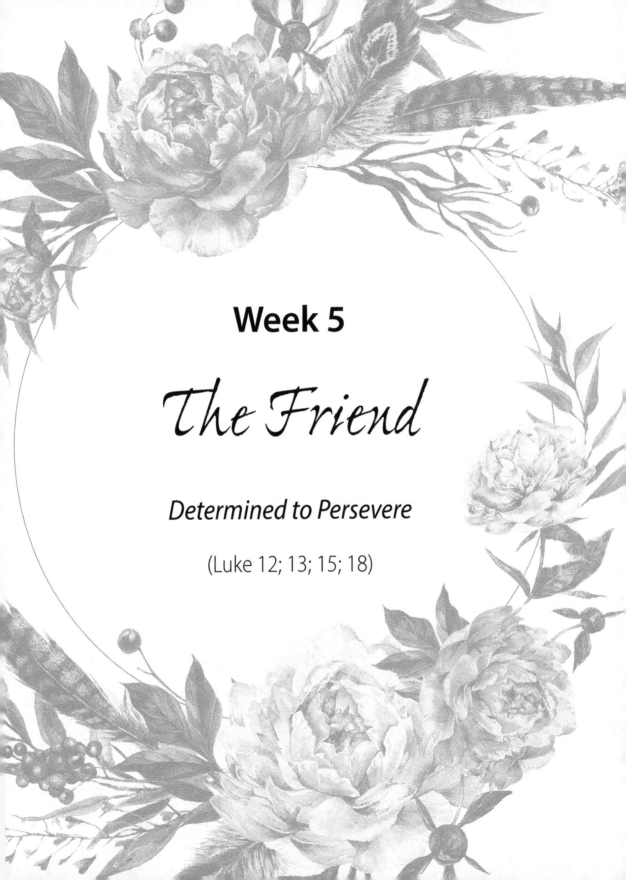

Week 5

The Friend

Determined to Persevere

(Luke 12; 13; 15; 18)

Leader Prep

Focus Verse

Blessed is the one who perseveres under trial because, having stood the test, that person will receive the crown of life that the Lord has promised to those who love him.

(James 1:12)

Scripture Highlights

Day 1

¹³*Someone in the crowd said to him, "Teacher, tell my brother to divide the inheritance with me."*

¹⁴*Jesus replied, "Man, who appointed me a judge or an arbiter between you?"* ¹⁵*Then he said to them, "Watch out! Be on your guard against all kinds of greed; life does not consist in an abundance of possessions."*

(Luke 12:13-15)

Day 2

²²*"Do not worry about your life, what you will eat; or about your body, what you will wear.* ²³*For life is more than food, and the body more than clothes.*

³¹ *. . . But seek his kingdom, and these things will be given to you as well."*

(Luke 12:22-23, 31)

Day 3

³¹*At that time some Pharisees came to Jesus and said to him, "Leave this place and go somewhere else. Herod wants to kill you."*

³²*He replied, "Go tell that fox, 'I will keep on driving out demons and healing people today and tomorrow, and on the third day I will reach my goal.'* ³³*In any case, I must press on today and tomorrow and the next day."*

(Luke 13:31-33a)

Day 4

¹¹*"There was a man who had two sons.* ¹²*The younger one said to his father, 'Father, give me my share of the estate.' So he divided his property between them.*

¹³*"Not long after that, the younger son got together all he had, set off for a distant country and there squandered his wealth in wild living. . . .*

¹⁷"When he came to his senses, he said, ... ¹⁸I will set out and go back to my father and say to him: Father, I have sinned against heaven and against you. ¹⁹I am no longer worthy to be called your son; make me like one of your hired servants.' ²⁰So he got up and went to his father.

"But while he was still a long way off, his father saw him and was filled with compassion for him; he ran to his son, threw his arms around him and kissed him....

²⁵"Meanwhile, the older son was in the field. When he came near the house, he heard music and dancing. ²⁶So he called one of the servants and asked him what was going on. ²⁷'Your brother has come,' he replied, 'and your father has killed the fattened calf because he has him back safe and sound.'

²⁸"The older brother became angry and refused to go in."

(Luke 15:11-13,17-20, 25-28)

Day 5

¹⁰"Two men went up to the temple to pray, one a Pharisee and the other a tax collector. ¹¹The Pharisee stood by himself and prayed: 'God, I thank you that I am not like other people—robbers, evildoers, adulterers—or even like this tax collector. ¹²I fast twice a week and give a tenth of all I get.'

¹³"But the tax collector stood at a distance. He would not even look up to heaven, but beat his breast and said, 'God, have mercy on me, a sinner.'

¹⁴"I tell you that this man, rather than the other, went home justified before God. For all those who exalt themselves will be humbled, and those who humble themselves will be exalted."

(Luke 18:10-14)

Materials Needed

- Determined DVD and DVD player
- Stick-on name tags and markers (optional)

Session Outline

Note: Refer to the format templates on page 6 for suggested time allotments.

Welcome and Opening Prayer

Offer a word of welcome to the group and a brief opening prayer, asking God to prepare the group to receive His Word and hear His voice.

Icebreaker

Invite the women to share short responses to the following question:

- How or where do you need perseverance in your life right now?

Video

Two short video segments are provided for Week 5. You are encouraged to begin with the group-centering video to help participants slow down internally, disconnect from the distractions of their busy lives, and center their hearts on God and God's Word. Then play the content video segment, which distills and recaps the main takeaways of the week's lessons. Invite participants to complete the Video Viewer Guide for Week 5 in the participant book as they watch (page 169). (Answers are provided on page 200 of the participant workbook and 63 of this leader guide.)

Group Discussion

Video Discussion Questions

- What does it mean to be a friend to the world? What are some opportunities you have to be a friend to the world?

Participant Book Discussion Questions

Note: More questions are provided than you will have time to cover. Put a check mark beside those you would like your group to discuss. Page references are provided for those questions that relate to questions or activities in the participant book.

Day 1: Ready to Live

- Read Luke 12:16-21 aloud. What are the priorities of the rich man in this parable? (page 143)
- What do you enjoy most about life, and what brings life the most meaning? (page 140)

- Review the three types of biblical inheritance on pages 141–143. How would you describe our spiritual inheritance shared with Christ?
- According to John 3:16, what is the most important inheritance for every believer? Describe what it feels like to receive this wonderful gift. (page 144)
- We don't have to wait until we get to heaven to tangibly experience some of that treasure. What rewards has walking with Jesus brought you? (Refer to your answers on page 144.)

Notes:

Day 2: Finding Peace by Straigtening Our Priorities

- Read aloud Luke 12:22-34. What does Jesus tell us not to do, and why? (page 147)
- Our priorities determine our peace. The by-product for placing worldly concerns over spiritual ones is worry. What are your top concerns—those things that bring you the most anxiety? (page 147) What are your top priorities right now?
- Would you say you have more worry or more peace about your priorities? Why?
- Read Philippians 4:8-9. What does it mean to "set our minds"? Do you find it easy or difficult to set your mind on things above when the things all around you bring anxiety and worry? How do we learn to set our minds above?

Notes:

Day 3: On Being Steadfast

- Have you experienced a situation in which you wanted to give up? Did you keep going and finish the task? If so, what kept you from walking away? (page 153)

- Read Luke 13:31-35 aloud. How do we see Jesus' compassion in these verses?
- What is your heart broken for in our world right now, or maybe in your own circle? How can you bring the compassion of Christ into those situations?
- Where is Jesus calling you today? (page 156)

Notes:

Day 4: Living with Grace

- What is your understanding of biblical *grace*? Refer to your simple definition on page 158 as well as the defining attributes you listed on page 161.
- Review the parable of the prodigal son and compare the three characters, referring to the chart on pages 158–159. Would you put yourself in the role of the younger son, the father, or the older son? Why?
- When has God shown you abundant grace? (page 159)
- Do you think people can ever be "too far gone" to be rescued? Why or why not? What does this story tell us about God's position on who is worthy of rescue?

Notes:

Day 5: Redefining Humility

- Read Luke 18:9-14 aloud. How would you compare the tax collector and Pharisee in these veres?
- On a scale of 1-10, with 1 being the least and 10 being the most, how would you rate the tax collector's dependence on God? (page 166) The Phairsee's dependence on God? (page 165)

- How easy or difficult is it for you to depend on God? (page 167) What does dependence on God mean for your daily life?
- Read Philippians 2:5-11. What does this passage teach us about humility?
- Why do you think humility often has a negative perception in our culture? Would you say that sometimes strength is required to show humility? Explain your thoughts.

Notes:

Determined Conversation

Divide into groups of 2-3 for the following:

- How is Jesus calling you to love the broken? Share the commitment you wrote on page 156, and pray for one another that Jesus would break your hearts for those around you who need His hope and healing. Ask Him to make you steadfast in your commitment to live and love as He did.

Prayer Requests

Close the session by taking personal prayer requests from group members and leading the group in prayer. Encourage members to participate in the Closing Prayer by praying out loud for one another and the requests given.

Week 6

The Victor

*Determined to Live
with Courage*

(Luke 19; 20; 22–24)

Leader Prep

Focus Verse

The one who says he remains in him should walk just as he walked.

(1 John 2:6 CSB)

Scripture Highlights

Day 1

[30]"Go to the village ahead of you, and as you enter it, you will find a colt tied there, which no one has ever ridden. Untie it and bring it here…."

[35]They brought it to Jesus, threw their cloaks on the colt and put Jesus on it. [36]As he went along, people spread their cloaks on the road.

[37]When he came near the place where the road goes down the Mount of Olives, the whole crowd of disciples began joyfully to praise God in loud voices for all the miracles they had seen:

[38]"Blessed is the king who comes in the name of the Lord!"

"Peace in heaven and glory in the highest!"

(Luke 19:30, 35-38)

Day 2

[9]"A man planted a vineyard, rented it to some farmers and went away for a long time. [10]At harvest time he sent a servant to the tenants so they would give him some of the fruit of the vineyard. But the tenants beat him and sent him away empty-handed. [11]He sent another servant, but that one also they beat and treated shamefully and sent away empty-handed. [12]He sent still a third, and they wounded him and threw him out.

[13]"Then the owner of the vineyard said, 'What shall I do? I will send my son, whom I love; perhaps they will respect him.'

[14]"But when the tenants saw him, they talked the matter over. 'This is the heir,' they said. 'Let's kill him, and the inheritance will be ours.' [15]So they threw him out of the vineyard and killed him.

"What then will the owner of the vineyard do to them? [16]He will come and kill those tenants and give the vineyard to others."

(Luke 20:9-16)

<u>Day 3</u>

47While he was still speaking a crowd came up, and the man who was called Judas, one of the Twelve, was leading them. He approached Jesus to kiss him, 48but Jesus asked him, "Judas, are you betraying the Son of Man with a kiss?"

49When Jesus' followers saw what was going to happen, they said, "Lord, should we strike with our swords?" 50And one of them struck the servant of the high priest, cutting off his right ear.

51But Jesus answered, "No more of this!" And he touched the man's ear and healed him.

(Luke 22:47-51)

<u>Day 4</u>

44It was now about noon, and darkness came over the whole land until three in the afternoon, 45for the sun stopped shining. And the curtain of the temple was torn in two. 46Jesus called out with a loud voice, "Father, into your hands I commit my spirit." When he had said this, he breathed his last.

(Luke 23:44-46)

<u>Day 5</u>

1On the first day of the week, very early in the morning, the women took the spices they had prepared and went to the tomb. 2They found the stone rolled away from the tomb, 3but when they entered, they did not find the body of the Lord Jesus. 4While they were wondering about this, suddenly two men in clothes that gleamed like lightning stood beside them. 5In their fright the women bowed down with their faces to the ground, but the men said to them, "Why do you look for the living among the dead? 6He is not here; he has risen! Remember how he told you, while he was still with you in Galilee: 7'The Son of Man must be delivered over to the hands of sinners, be crucified and on the third day be raised again.' " 8Then they remembered his words.

9When they came back from the tomb, they told all these things to the Eleven and to all the others.

(Luke 24:1-9)

Materials Needed
* Determined DVD and DVD player
* Stick-on name tags and markers (optional)

Session Outline

Note: Refer to the format templates on page 6 for suggested time allotments.

Welcome and Opening Prayer

Offer a word of welcome to the group and a brief opening prayer, asking God to prepare the group to receive His Word and hear His voice.

Icebreaker

Invite the women to share short responses to the following question:

- What is something you've done that required great courage?

Video

Two short video segments are provided for Week 6. You are encouraged to begin with the group-centering video to help participants slow down internally, disconnect from the distractions of their busy lives, and center their hearts on God and God's Word. Then play the content video segment, which distills and recaps the main takeaways of the week's lessons. Invite participants to complete the Video Viewer Guide for Week 6 in the participant book as they watch (page 199). (Answers are provided on page 200 of the participant workbook and 63 of this leader guide.)

Group Discussion

Video Discussion Questions

- How are you continuing the ongoing work of Jesus' ministry?
- What choices are you going to make to live like Jesus?

Participant Book Discussion Questions

Note: More questions are provided than you will have time to cover. Put a check mark beside those you would like your group to discuss. Page references are provided for those questions that relate to questions or activities in the participant book.

Day 1: Defiance and Courage

- Have you ever felt that the details of your life are insignificant to God? If so, explain why. (page 174)
- Can you recall a time when you've seen God's hand in the details of your life? If so, share briefly. (page 175)

- Read Luke 19:41 aloud. What is Jesus' response as He approaches Jerusalem? We have seen Jesus' compassion for Jerusalem previously in Luke 13. Why do you think He weeps now? (page 175)
- What range of feelings must Jesus have experienced as He rode into Jerusalem on a donkey, knowing full well what was to come? How can Jesus' example help us as determined living takes us into situations that seem hopeless?
- Would you describe yourself as courageous? Why or why not? How do we gain courage to follow God into impossible and hopeless situations?

Notes:

Day 2: Grace Under Pressure
- How would you describe the way you handle conflict? What do you find most challenging about facing conflict? (page 179)
- Read Luke 20:2 aloud. What question do the chief priests, teachers of the law, and elders ask of Jesus? What is the root of their opposition with Jesus? (page 179)
- Refer to your notes on page 180 regarding Jesus' response when challenged. What did you discover from these situations about the way Jesus handles conflict?
- We will face rejection and opposition as we seek to live like Jesus. How can we determine to choose love and display grace under pressure when conflict arises? What does grace under pressure look like in real life?

Notes:

Day 3: Changed for Good
- Read Luke 22:39-46 aloud. What does Jesus' time of prayer in the garden teach us about facing suffering?

- How does Luke 22:45-53 show us that Jesus was determined to obey His Father's will regardless?
- Can you recall a time when you felt like you were facing difficulty alone? If so, describe it briefly. (page 185) Did you experience the strength of God in that situation, and if so, how?
- If you don't mind sharing, is God asking you to move forward with something today that you don't want to do? Does moving forward in His will mean that you will have to sacrifice one of your desires? What gives you strength and courage for moving forward?

Notes:

Day 4: The Power of the Breath

- Take turns reading aloud Genesis 2:7; Job 33:4; Psalm 103:29-30; Isaiah 42:5; and Ezekiel 37:5-6. What do these verses say about the breath of God? (page 191) How does God's breath fill us and sustain us?
- Do you ever find yourself feeling out of breath with all you're carrying or facing? How might remembering your breath with intention help to sustain you through these times?
- What comes to mind when you hear this statement? Intentionally living like Jesus means that nothing is wasted and everything is precious. How can you open your eyes to what each day holds for you?

Notes:

Day 5: Witness to Life

- Read Luke 24:1-12. Consider all that these women have seen over the three years of Jesus' ministry. What stories do you think have stayed with them the most? What about Jesus do you think they would be most eager to share with their friends and family? (page 194)

- What about your life with Jesus are you most eager to share with others?
- Which lessons from our study have resonated most with you? Refer to the chart on pages 195–196.

Notes:

Determined Conversation

Divide into groups of 2-3 for the following:

- Over the past six weeks, how have you embraced intentional, abundant life? How are you determined to live like Jesus in every moment? (page 198)

Prayer Requests

Close the session by taking personal prayer requests from group members and leading the group in prayer. You might encourage members to participate in the Closing Prayer by praying out loud for one another and the requests given.

VIDEO VIEWER GUIDE ANSWERS

Week 1

choose life

wandering aimlessly

choices

Week 2

hearts

truth

know

Week 3

asleep

in control

faith / fears

Week 4

rescue

endurance

sacrifice / blessing

Week 5

need

honor

ignore / abandon

Week 6

hope / return

joy

continues

CPSIA information can be obtained
at www.ICGtesting.com
Printed in the USA
LVHW011150050920
665016LV00002B/2